T0149407

Slices of Life

of

A Solo Existence of a Universal Artist

Katie Waters

BALBOA.
PRESS

A DIVISION OF HAY HOUSE

Balboa Press books may be ordered through booksellers or by contacting:

Balboa Press
A Division of Hay House
1663 Liberty Drive
Bloomington, IN 47403
www.balboapress.com.au
1 (877) 407-4847

Print information available on the last page.

ISBN: 978-1-5043-0745-1 (sc)
ISBN: 978-1-5043-0744-4 (e)

Balboa Press rev. date: 04/11/2017

Contents

1. Chosen 1

2. The Adopted One.. 3

3. The Dark Years 5

4. My Wild Years 9

5. Questions and Answers...................................... 13

6. The Tunnel.. 15

7. The Step... 17

8. I Shower My Love upon Mother Earth 19

9. I Fell in Love with You 21

10. To My Brother.. 23

11. New Age Dawners 25

12. The Land of My Heart....................................... 27

13. The Passing of My Son 31

14. Interconnected 35

For my wonderful daughter and son.
You will always be my world and inspiration.

Introduction

Katie Waters was born in Victoria, Australia. The name of this book *Slices of Life,* is exactly what it is about: slices of Katie's life. Katie is grateful for all the lessons that have crossed her path in life so far: forgiveness, strength, courage, wisdom, and understanding. A real solo existence of a universal artist.

She keeps in the back of her mind that one day, her poetry will inspire, enlighten and awaken as many people as possible in their life journeys. Katie has always been passionate about caring for people and the planet, and she continues contributing still to this day.

Chosen

l was only together with my family
for a short while.
My mother was killed.
My family was shattered.
l was just a small child.

My father was brave; to a new land
they had come,
to start a new life; it had barely just begun.
He went back
to the faraway land, left two of us behind.
Into a home for adoption we went,
to find families loving and kind.

A year passed; l was lined up
with all the others,
white dress,
socks, and shoes,
and stood there, patiently waiting.

They paced and looked along the line
to choose which one.
l raised my arms to be picked up.
l was chosen,
then taken home to meet my new brothers
and family.
A whole new life had begun.

The Adopted One

l embraced my new life:
a loving family,
sharing of happiness and fun.
A home with a dog,
a lot of new friends,
a kind ghost in my room,
playtime in fresh air,
water, and sun.

My parents worked hard
for all that we had.
How happy l was
to have a mum and dad.
No help from their families
did they get. l was labelled
"the Adopted One";
how could l ever forget?

The Dark Years

At last, I was off to school
at the age of nearly five.
I was so excited,
ready, willing, and feeling
very much alive.
My primary years
were the darkest years;
a real living nightmare was to unfold.
My parents believed
they were doing the right thing,
sending me through
private religious education.

Stripped of my confidence,
my personality and self-esteem crushed,
through humiliation,
physical cruelty,
and verbal abuse.
I was repeatedly
punched, hit, shoved,
whacked, and slapped.
Humiliated, shouted, and yelled at
in front of others, till l cried.
Told l was a sinner:
"l will never be good enough,"
"l would be struck dead
if l didn't go to church on Sundays,"

and the list goes on.
I witnessed the cruelty and abuse
towards others as well.
I wondered why.
"If God loved us so much,
why did he do this to his sheep?"
To stand up and question this,
l did do dare, with a spat of anger
I was told to "sit in the corner and
write a hundred lines,"
followed by a deadly stare.

The nuns would laugh and smile
when the parents
were in view.
The children would look up to their faces,
knowing
there were two.

My Wild Years

My secondary years were my wild years,
still in the
private religious education.
I had no respect left for the nuns
or for any other of the teachers
by this stage, or the whole
religious situation.

l could do the work, but
l didn't apply any effort.
l despised the religious lessons
with a passion.
I saw it all being so cruel,
dishonest, hateful, and a
breeding ground of fear.
I would be disruptive and
cheeky. I'd wag school, and
my friends did the same.

I had to find a way out,
away from this religious sect.
They would speak of
love and respect but
practised the opposite.
I didn't belong with these people;
no wonder l went wild.
Where is the real
love and respect in this world,
which l deserve?
There was a desire in my heart
to find peace;

there is a lot more to life than this.
I walked away from it all,
to my family's
outrage and disgust.
I was grateful
for my parents' hard work
and good intentions, but
I couldn't live this sectarian
way of life.
So walking away
to find myself was a must.

I ran amuck for awhile
with different groups.
l began working for artisans
and learning their crafts.
I tried to help with saving the whales,
the forests, and the trees.
I wanted to find a
freedom in myself, to be happy,
to learn to feel me again.

I felt an inner calling,
a feeling l couldn't resist.
You never know
how life will turn.
I transformed myself into a
proud and caring nurse.
I always knew, deep inside,
caring for all living things
was my passion.

Questions and Answers

Who am I?
What am I?
Where do I come from?
I am who I am.
I can listen to my heart for what.
I began from an existence
which has always been.
Through this journey of learning,
which has the need of existence, I will return
to what will always be.

The Tunnel

Two and a half days in labour,
I finally gave birth the natural way.
Suddenly, a medical emergency occurred,
I could feel myself
slowly passing.

With incredible speed, l was being pulled along
in a tunnel, towards a
pulsating white light,
the brightest
you will ever see.

I felt an overwhelming
joy and peacefulness.
Then an angel whispered,
"It's not your time."

I awoke two days later; the doctor said,
"We almost lost you."

The Step

Confusion, seclusion, life knowledge with everydayness.
The smile of the evil and the cunning at work.
The wisdom to know who's the real jerk.

The destructiveness of use and abuse,
times of struggle and bleak.
I've stood at an edge, to confront the deceit.

Shall l flip a coin and join, and be part
of the misleading and mistrusted?
I look back knowing my thoughts,
feeling deep within myself,
rather disgusted.

I Shower My Love upon Mother Earth

My soul searches for enlightenment;
the direction and inspiration l have received,
from the universe to within, l feel it so strong,
like mountains upon my skin.
I shower my love upon Mother Earth.

I feel like an opened flower, stretching to the sun,
in a field, crowded by many.
Filling the air with an energy of goodwill and love,
helping others on their journey, towards the heavens above.
I shower my love and thankfulness upon Mother Earth.

We dance with love in our hearts and rejoice,
when in this harmony, we listen to our inner voice.
We take the hands of our brothers and sisters with love
and go another step forward to our heaven above.
I shower my love upon Mother Earth.

I Fell in Love with You

I had the destiny to have met you,
awakened another step forward
on my journey in life, that
spiritual love does exist.

Our time together l feel is enlightening
and precious in my heart.
Our time apart, feelings of fear and doubt
make one unhappy,
incomplete, or unsure.

If only the heart could be felt,
the mouth would
only speak words of truth,
the eyes would
see with clarity,
and the hands would
take hold of the caring.

Have you the time to realize,
another exists
in your life?

My heart has felt the yearn of its existence.
I have no more fear and doubt, a loved friend
in my life forever.

To My Brother

Even though you may feel
everything is upon your shoulders,
and your soul is breaking,
be aware that this well of darkness
is the dawn of a new awakening.
You may feel your intelligence
is being insulted
and your world has crumbled;
be strong and wise, my brother, and
love yourself.

We will walk with you upon this earth.
You're not mad, crazy, or out of your mind.
Your one of the most beautiful souls,
who's caring, loving, and kind.
It's heartbreaking and sad to see
that through your eyes,
you can only see fickled,
simply because
you keep yourself pickled.

New Age Dawners

We have opened the doors of our hearts for one another,
to love, to learn, and to respect our global Mother.
Things cannot be awakened and changed overnight,
to seek and feel the eternal universal light.

I bow my head to the white light, my arms raised
towards the sun, to ask for the blessed energy to
flow down upon everyone.
The love and light to be given in all the world's corners,
the awakening of souls of the New Age dawners.

The Land of My Heart

I came unto you on a beautiful day gone past,
l was blessed with a land of glory,
sunshine, and blue skies that last.
You gave to me all that l needed to grow.
I now return that beauty; l now know.

From the deep, cold, starry skies by night,
from the distant warm sun bringing its light.
The caring and sharing of my soul sings,
the loving and giving the land of my heart brings.

The rhythm of life brings its sadness and joy,
as part of the deal.
But it's what we need to show us exactly what's real.
If it wasn't for the struggle and confusion as we know,
we wouldn't understand the peace to grow.

From the deep, cold, starry skies by night,
from the distant warm sun bringing its light.
The caring and sharing of my soul sings,
the loving and giving the land of my heart brings.

If it wasn't for the other, your sister and brother,
I now do speak, you would not have a purpose
of anything and nothing to seek.
So now we see what we need to give
to us, the people,
our land, in which we live.

From the deep, cold, starry skies by night,
From the distant warm sun bringing its light.
The caring and sharing of my soul sings,
The loving and giving the land of my heart brings.

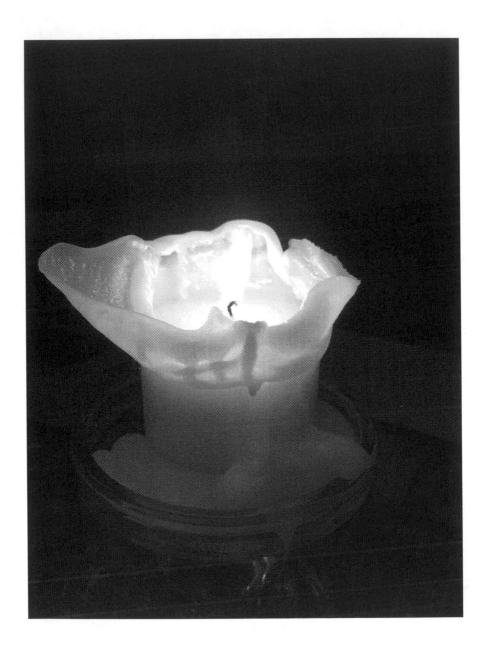

The Passing of My Son

I was told "in an accident," my son Odin had passed.
I felt a heavy thump just below my chest.
I took some steps back in disbelief;
the room began to shrink.
My mind was only thinking,
No, no, it isn't true!
I stood and just cried,
"It must be someone else!"
When my senses came back into a sort of balance,
I realized it was true.
I went numb. My life had shattered.

How can a mother find words to express
her deepest sorrow?
It's something
I'll never recover from, but
the strong can adjust in time.
The healing process has begun; it can take years.

So many tears were shed, and then came
the dry tears, which l didn't even know existed.
Life seems surreal.
You only hear,
see, and feel what you need.
Your mind and body had gone into
survival mode. I will never be the same again.
I had an inner fear of going over an edge.
I've had to feel life deeply, to grow stronger.

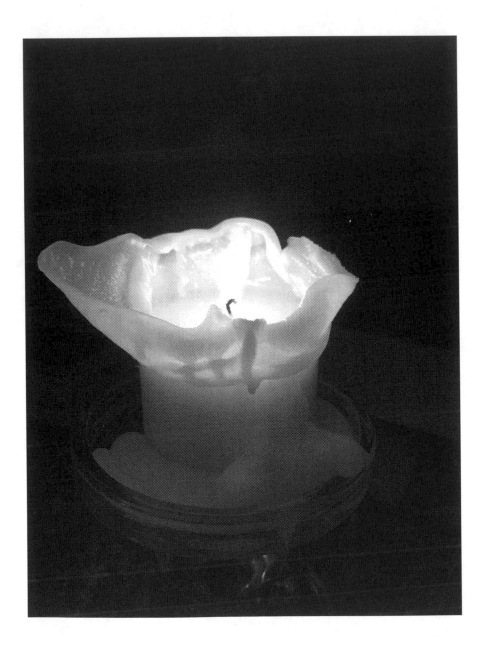

A short time passed. l went back to work
as a nurse to keep myself grounded.
Helping others at their worst gave me the strength
to keep going.
I needed them as much as they needed me.
Every free moment l would think of my son Odin,
a wonderful and unique soul.
I still do.
I feel honoured and grateful
to be his mother.

Interconnected

We are all interconnected:
people,
plants,
animals,
water,
air,
and the list goes on.
We survive only because of one another.
We are all part of one.

The darkness has shown us
the light,
the moon, and the stars,
the good that is in our world,
which has helped us to grow.
There are the souls who only know
the darkness, and
so it is.

The lightness has shown us
the beautiful,
colourful, and wondrous planet
in which we live.
The courage,
the strength,
the wisdom we have grown to know
so we can
love and respect all living things.
We are all interconnected.
And
so it is.

About the Author

Katie Waters was born in Victoria, Australia, and began writing poetry in 1987.

Katie is a visionary, a mystic, and a poet. From as far back as she can remember, she has always been passionate about caring for all living things. Throughout her life, she has always cared for people, animals, and nature, and she continues still to this day.

Slices of Life has been a dream come true; Katie wants to make a contribution towards enlightening the lives of as many people as possible.

Love and light.

Printed in the United States
By Bookmasters